Copyright © 2025 by Lashawnda Shiree Love

All rights reserved. No part of this publication may be reproduced, stored in a retrieval system, or transmitted in any form or by any means—electronic, mechanical, photocopying, recording, or otherwise—without prior written permission from the publisher, except for brief quotations used in reviews or scholarly works.

Published by:
Stork Publishing LLC
Email: storkpublishingllc@gmail.com

Designed and formatted by:
Intellectual Designs by Lashawnda Love
Email: intellectualdesigns20@gmail.com
Website: www.lashawndashiree.info/the-love-lab-design-and-publish
Phone: 334-232-9281
Location: Bainbridge, Georgia

All articles, cover design, and layout were created by Intellectual Designs by Lashawnda Love.

Photo Acknowledgment:
All personal images featured throughout this publication were voluntarily submitted by the individuals and couples featured in this edition. Permission was granted by each party for publication and use solely within this magazine. These images remain the property of the original owners and may not be reused or redistributed without their written consent.

For inquiries, services, or collaborations, please contact us using the information provided above.

Printed in the United States of America.

7-11 Nicole Smith

13-14 H.E. Denisa Gokovi

16-18 Meet Lashawnda Love

21-68 Faith Tales & Transformation

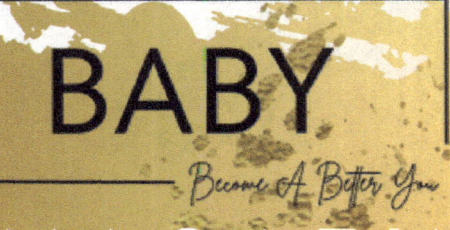

BABY
Become A Better You

MAGAZINE 2025

70-72 Harmony Hynms

75-86 Rising Stars

Welcome to the 7th Edition of Magazine!

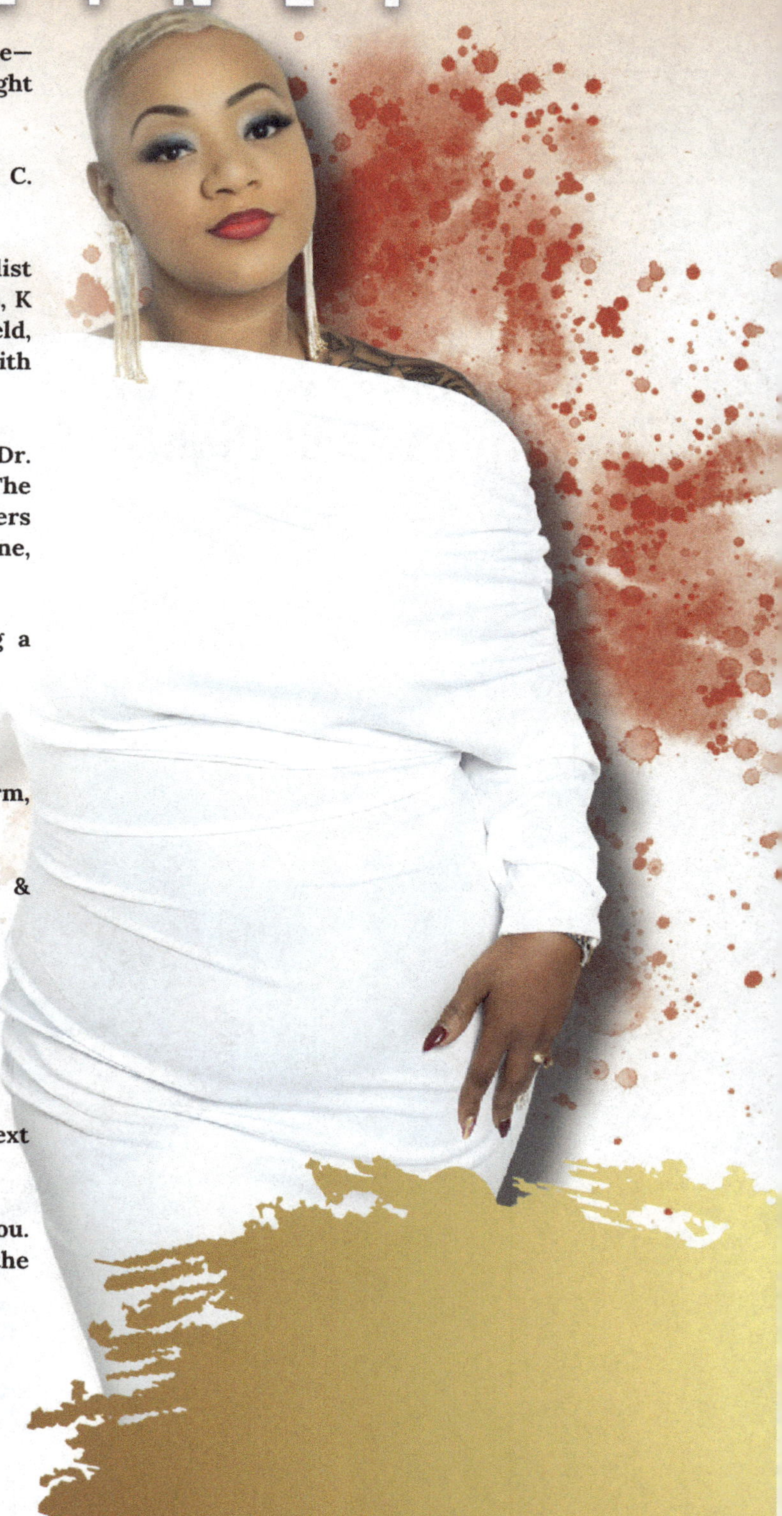

Welcome to the Christmas Edition 2025 of B.A.B.Y. Magazine—our 8th powerful release, created to inspire, uplift, and spotlight the extraordinary gifts within our community.

This special edition features H.E. Denisa Gokovi and Nicole C. Smith, with H.E. Denisa Gokovi gracing our front cover.

From influential voices such as Keiaundria Ragland, Evangelist Atiya Jenkins, Dr. YaQuanda Payne-McCall, Jeremerica Jones, K Free & Free Flow, to our rising kidpreneurs Germani Bromfield, Purpose Lamb, and Malaysia Thomas, this edition is filled with purpose-driven excellence spanning generations.

You'll also find powerful contributions from Dora Black, Dr. Wallace C. Cooper, Porsha Hunt, YaQuanda McCall, and The Draggs. We proudly highlight the impact of dynamic leaders including Janet Love, Elder Tonya Rose, Dr. Oswalyn Simone, Viola Flanders, Stacie Rogers, and Delesa Patterson.

Don't miss our special feature, "Meet the Loves," offering a deeper look into the hearts and vision behind this movement.

Inside This Edition

This issue unfolds across impactful sections designed to inform, inspire, and empower:

Ministry Stories, Bios & Testimonies — Faith Tales & Transformation
Stories of divine breakthrough, resilience, and purpose.

Gospel Music — Harmony Hymns
Uplifting melodies and lyrics that speak directly to the soul.

Youth & Young Adults — Rising Stars
Celebrating bold talent and trailblazers shaping the next generation.

To every contributor, reader, and featured guest—thank you. Your support fuels our mission to uplift lives and celebrate the journey of Becoming a Better You.

With love and anticipation,

Lashawnda Love
Editors-in-Chief, B.A.B.Y. Magazine

NICOLE C.

A Fighter's Faith and Her Journey from Grief to Purpose

BY LASHAWNDA SHIREE LOVE

"No matter what life has thrown at me, I let my faith in God be bigger."

In a world that often underestimates the quiet resilience of women, Nicole C. Smith stands as a beacon of faith, courage, and unwavering determination. The author of A Woman's Sanctuary and Widows in the Wilderness, Smith's life story reads like a testament to the power of trusting God even in the most harrowing moments.

"I want the world to remember me by one simple word: Fighter," Smith says. "Because no matter what life has thrown at me, I let my faith in God be bigger." That faith, she explains, has been her anchor, especially after the tragic death of a close friend. "No one knew how it really affected my life," she shares, "but it drew me back and closer to God."

Her journey into writing was divinely guided. "First, I have to give God all the glory and credit," Smith says. "He spoke to my spirit and gave me the assignment to write and encourage others with these devotionals." It was through this calling that her first book, Widows in the Wilderness, came to life—a deeply personal reflection on grief after the death of her husband of 24 years. Smith recalls the challenge of processing such immense loss: "Some people felt that because I knew God and had faith, I shouldn't have been as hurt as I was. But God understood me, and that's why I am healed today."

Turning pain into purpose became her mission. By trusting God and embracing the writing process, Smith shared her story without hesitation or fear of judgment. "God turned my pain into purpose by trusting me to write and give my story. It was through that honesty that healing began," she reflects. Her favorite scripture, Proverbs 3:5-6, serves as a daily reminder: "When I put my trust in God, He will see me through. He can fix what I cannot."

SMITH

PERSEVERANCE IS ROOTED IN RESPONSIBILITY

For Smith, perseverance is rooted in responsibility—to her family, friends, and the readers who may one day draw strength from her words. "I had people depending on me. I could not fold. My children needed to see that God will see us through any situation," she explains. Today, the word "healing" resonates deeply with her as the process of being made whole.

Smith also shares practical wisdom for navigating life and ministry. "Over the years I had to learn balance," she says. "I give myself a schedule most days to do certain tasks. It keeps me grounded and on track." One God moment she will never forget was when she began writing her first book: "I had no idea how to start or what to say. I just began to pray and listen to the voice of God, and everything came to me naturally."

DO NOT WORRY

To those who feel invisible or overlooked, she offers heartfelt encouragement: "Do not worry. You may feel this way because of your own insecurities or because of people. But God sees you. Remain faithful to Him, and when the time is right, He will bring you to the front of the line." Her advice to aspiring writers is just as bold: "Just do it. Don't sugarcoat what you have been through. It's your story, and tell it with all you have in you. It will touch someone's life."

LEAVING A LEGACY

Leaving a legacy is deeply personal for Smith. "To me, it means leaving something important behind for my children, family, and friends to remember me by—like unwavering faith no matter what happens in life. It's more than material possessions." Worship, she adds, has been central to her spiritual strength. "True worship gives you an intimate one-on-one relationship with God. You cannot have a genuine worship experience and remain the same spiritually or emotionally. It strengthens you to handle life's challenges knowing God has your back."

HER PRAYER FOR EVERY READER OF HER BOOKS IS THAT THEY FIND STRENGTH AND COURAGE

In this season of life, Nicole C. Smith continues to draw closer to God, praying that her ministry and business prosper while inspiring others to live boldly in their faith. Her prayer for every reader of her books is that they find strength and courage in the midst of their own trials. "We never know what someone else is going through or suffering in silence," she reflects.

CONNECT WITH NICOLE C. SMITH

For those who wish to connect with Nicole C. Smith, she can be found on Facebook @Nicole C. Smith or reached by email at awomansanctuary@gmail.com. Her life, story, and unwavering faith remain a testimony that through God, pain can become purpose, grief can transform into guidance, and a fighter can leave an everlasting legacy.

> THE PERSON THAT CHALLENGES YOU AND HOLDS YOU ACCOUNTABLE LOVES YOU MORE THAN THE PERSON THAT WATCHES YOU STAY THE SAME AND SETTLE FOR MEDIOCRITY.

GOD TURNED MY PAIN INTO PURPOSE BY

TRUSTING ME
WITH MY STORY

BOOK ALERT

NOW ON AUDIO
audible

PUT YOUR CAT ON THE ALTAR

AUTHOR
Lashawnda Love

GET YOUR COPY TODAY!
 amazon 🌐 www.lashawndashiree.info/books

H. E. DENISA GOKOVI
COMPOSING A LEGACY OF ART, ADVOCACY, AND GLOBAL IMPACT

H. E. Denisa Gokovi stands at the intersection of music, humanitarian leadership, and global advocacy. With a Master of Arts in Music Theory and Composition from the University of Arts in Albania, she has built a career that transcends performance, positioning herself as both a cultural force and a voice for social transformation.

Recognized as one of Albania's leading pianists, Denisa's excellence is reflected in the numerous national and international awards she has earned throughout her career. Yet, her work extends far beyond concert halls. She is deeply committed to nurturing the next generation of artists, dedicating time and expertise to the professional development and training of young musicians.

Her influence was recently highlighted during a conference and festival in Albania, where she collaborated with emerging dancer Geraldine Gryka. Together, their artistic presentation resonated with young audiences, demonstrating how creativity and humanity can intersect to inspire hope and purpose.

Alongside her artistic achievements, Denisa is widely respected for her humanitarian efforts. She actively participates in initiatives at both national and international levels, with a particular focus on protecting and advancing the rights of women and children. She remains closely affiliated with one of Albania's most established organizations, the Association For the Benefit of Albanian Women, where she works collaboratively to promote integrity, development, and empowerment.

Through this association, Denisa also supports a music education initiative that provides free instruction to women and abandoned children. This program is designed not only to foster artistic expression, but also to strengthen psychological resilience and create pathways toward economic stability.

Denisa's advocacy has positioned her as a respected voice in global forums. She has been invited to speak at numerous conferences, representing underprivileged communities and addressing social and diplomatic challenges. Her perspectives have been featured across television, magazines, and newspapers, further amplifying her mission on an international scale.

Her leadership roles are extensive and distinguished. She has received honors such as the Global Humanitarian Award from the World Peace & Diplomacy Organization and has served as Chairperson and Speaker for Albania at the Women's Economic Forum in India. Additionally, she has held positions within global human rights and sustainability initiatives, including ECO LEAGUE Forums and Cher Eco City in Singapore.

Beyond titles and accolades, Denisa identifies herself as a Musician, Writer, and Philosopher. She views creativity as a responsibility—one that carries the power to reflect pivotal moments, challenge injustice, and cultivate dialogue across cultures. Whether through music or the written word, her work consistently centers on knowledge, human values, and the exchange of meaningful ideas within international audiences.

Her journey began in Shkoder, Albania, a city rich in cultural heritage but marked by economic hardship. Trained in piano from an early age, Denisa performed in competitions and festivals throughout her childhood, earning recognition while navigating personal and familial adversity caused by systemic corruption. These early challenges shaped her resilience and ignited a lifelong commitment to humanism, justice, and leadership.

Today, Denisa continues to collaborate with global organizations focused on culture, peace, and prosperity. Through her ambassadorial roles, she champions ethical leadership, artistic expression, and social responsibility. For her, being an ambassador is not symbolic—it is an active commitment to improving lives and shaping a more equitable global narrative.

At the core of Denisa Gokovi's work is a driving passion: building sustainable ideas, fostering professional integrity, and using creativity as a bridge between cultures. Her legacy is still being written, but its foundation is already clear—one rooted in courage, compassion, and an unwavering belief in the transformative power of art.

"Creativity is not only expression—it is responsibility. Through art, we reflect truth, challenge injustice, and shape the legacy we leave behind."
— H. E. Denisa Gokovi

Stork Publishing

OFFERS THE FOLLOWING SERVICES:

- GHOSTWRITING
- EDITING
- PUBLISHING
- PERSONALIZED JOURNALS
- PERSONALIZED NOTEBOOKS
- PERSONALIZED PLANNERS
- PERSONALIZED EBOOKS
- MAGAZINES
- CALENDARS

Lashawnda Love

334-232-9281

@thelovelab

Lashawnda Shiree Love: A Journey of Faith, Creativity, and Empowerment

Lashawnda Shiree Love embodies the spirit of versatility, resilience, and passion. As a devoted wife, loving mother, entrepreneur, minister, author, and community service provider, Lashawnda's multifaceted talents have made a significant impact in various fields. Her journey is a testament to her unwavering faith, creativity, and commitment to helping others.

Family and Faith

Lashawnda is married to David Hassan Habbi Love and is the proud mother of three children: Chadrick Kyles Jr., 24, Shedrick Kyles, 20, and Purpose Lamb, 10. Her family is the cornerstone of her life, providing the foundation for her numerous ventures. She combines her roles as a wife and mother with her deep faith, which fuels her dedication to community service and ministry.

Entrepreneurial Ventures

As the visionary founder of The Love Lab: Design & Publishing Co., Lashawnda Love has merged her dynamic brands—Intellectual Designs and Stork Publishing LLC—into one powerhouse entity dedicated to creativity, strategy, and purpose-driven execution. Through The Love Lab, Lashawnda specializes in social media marketing, brand development, website creation, graphic design, and author publishing services. Her creative genius has graced the pages and layouts of Mogul Leaders Magazine, N.B.Q. Magazine, and K.I.S.H. Magazine, where her magazine development and graphics have turned heads and elevated voices.

Beyond publishing and design, Lashawnda's entrepreneurial spirit extends into beauty with her signature cosmetics line, Lashawnda Shiree, featuring long-lasting 16-hour matte lipsticks and luxurious lip liners. Whether building bold brands, launching impactful books, or creating standout beauty products, Lashawnda continues to break barriers and inspire others to walk boldly in their calling.

Musical Talents

A gifted singer and songwriter, Lashawnda has produced several soul-stirring singles, including "Deeper," "The Perfect Gift," "Silent Night," and "Because of Who You Are." She also spearheaded the Prophetic Release "Prayer for the Nations" CD, further demonstrating her deep spiritual commitment.

LITERARY CONTRIBUTIONS

In the literary realm, Lashawnda Shiree Love has authored a powerful collection of books and devotionals that speak directly to the heart, mind, and spirit. Her most recent works include Back to School, Not Back to Stress: Teen Sunday School Curriculum – August Edition, Girl, Just Breathe and A Guide to Winning the War Against a Narcissist (Newly Updated Edition), No Love Me Like This, Help My Husband Has a Girlfriend: A Guide to Healing, Growth, and Clarity, When Choices Hurt: A Journey of Redemption from Domestic Violence, Run, Stop, End the Affair, Ask God for a Sign, and Prayer Changes Things: A Wife's Faithful Prayers. She has also penned Fruit of the Spirit: A 3-Day Vacation Bible School Program, SoulSync: 30 Days of Love and Prayer, Put Your Cat on the Altar, Breakthrough: A 6-Week Journey for Women to Overcome Challenges, Rock Your Spouse's World: 7 Days Out of the Month, Make Your Marriage Better (Free eBook), and The Loves Marriage Matters Notebook Collection. Her collaborative work includes A Girl's Guide to Purity, co-authored with Dr. Erica Thomas. As a gifted ghostwriter, she brought to life her husband's testimony in How I Went from Arrested to Rescued, his devotional 30 Days of Transformation: Overcoming Addiction and Embracing a New Life, and her daughter's empowering children's book Hey, My Name is Purpose and I Love My Hair. Lashawnda is also the visionary behind B.A.B.Y. Magazine, having released six powerful editions including the 1st Edition, 2nd Edition (Christmas), 3rd Edition (Mother's Day), 4th Edition (Fall), the Marriage Edition 2025, and the Summer Edition 2025 featuring Apostle Dr. Wallace C. Cooper Jr. Her agenda, Just a Girl Who Survived and Decided to Build Her Empire, stands as a bold testament to her resilience, faith, and purpose-driven mission.

EMPOWERING THE COMMUNITY

Through The Loves Collection, a beautiful blend of journals, notebooks, and inspirational T-shirts, Lashawnda and her husband express their passion for purpose-filled living, love, and empowerment. Recently, Lashawnda unified her two powerhouse brands—Stork Publishing LLC and Intellectual Designs by Lashawnda Love—under one bold and creative umbrella: The Love Lab: Design & Publishing Co. This transformative hub was created to serve authors, visionaries, and entrepreneurs with excellence in branding, publishing, and content development. The Love Lab is not just a company; it's a movement—built with passion, branded by purpose.

Lashawnda Shiree Love is a radiant force of hope, creativity, and restoration. Her ability to wear many hats—author, editor, strategist, designer, therapist, wife, and mother—is matched only by her unwavering faith in God. Whether she's publishing life-changing books, helping others birth their visions, or building legacy through words and design, Lashawnda is living proof that you can overcome anything, build something beautiful from brokenness, and empower generations to come.

For More Information:

Email: lashawndashiree@gmail.com
Website: www.lashawndashiree.info
Social Media: Facebook (Lashawnda Shiree Love), Instagram (Lashawnda Love), and TikTok (Lashawnda Love).

In Loving Memories Of

Ervin B. Flanders Jr.

December 26, 1986 – October 28, 2012

REST IN PEACE ERVIN YOU ARE LOVED AND MISSED

Today, we remember and honor the life of Ervin, our beloved brother whose presence was both powerful and peaceful. He was the kind of man whose quiet strength anchored everyone around him—solid, dependable, and deeply loved. Ervin didn't need to be the loudest in the room to be the most respected. His wisdom, humility, and unwavering love for his family spoke volumes.

He loved deeply, laughed wholeheartedly, and lived with integrity. Whether it was through his gentle advice, his helping hands, or his ability to make you feel safe just by being there, Ervin left a mark that time will never erase.

Though our hearts are heavy, we know his legacy lives on in every life he touched. Heaven gained a good man—one we will forever cherish, celebrate, and carry with us.

Rest well, big brother. You ran your race with grace. We'll hold your memory close and your love even closer.

With love,
Your family.

Faith Tales & Transformation

SHENDORA "Rose Black"

R.I.H
R.I.H
R.I.H

"She walked in like she owned the room... and she did."

HER PEACE WAS EVERYTHING:

HONORING THE LIFE & LEGACY OF SHENDORA "ROSE BLACK"

Fall 2025 – Special Domestic Violence Awareness Edition

Shendora Black, lovingly known as "Rose," had a presence you couldn't ignore. She didn't just enter a room—she owned it. Her bubbly personality, warm energy, and unforgettable laugh made you feel like you were right where you belonged. To know her was to know joy. To be around her was to feel love.

Whether it was a family cookout, a phone call, or a random drop-in, Shendora showed up with her full heart. Her presence was magnetic. She didn't meet strangers—she met family. Her laughter would echo through a space and remind you to smile, even when life didn't give you much reason to.

Family was everything to her. The love she poured into her children was deep and unwavering, but her nurturing spirit didn't stop there. She was the auntie that everyone loved. Nieces, nephews, cousins, and kids in the neighborhood—no child was a stranger to her. Her arms were always open, and her home was always a place of comfort.

A MAMA, A DREAMER
A Fighter

Shendora "Rose" Black was more than a name in the community—she was a spirit that glowed with ambition, love, and purpose. She worked hard, dreamed big, and never stopped believing that better days were ahead. For her, the future wasn't just something to hope for; it was something to build with her own two hands.

One of Shendora's biggest dreams was to own her own trucking company. She talked about it often and with so much excitement that her family could almost see the logo already printed on the side of the trucks. She was simply waiting on her son, Tyiun, to graduate before taking that leap of faith. That dream wasn't just about financial freedom—it was about legacy. She wanted to create something that her children could look back on and say, "Mama did that."

Her family remembers how her eyes would light up when she spoke about her plans. Independence meant everything to her. She had a heart that refused to settle for less than peace. She talked about it often, reminding others, "Your peace is everything. Protect it." Those words were more than advice—they were the core of who she was.

What people remember most about Shendora is how deeply she cared. She was loyal to the bone, dependable to the core, and generous beyond measure. If you called, she'd answer. If you needed her, she'd come. No matter how busy life got, she somehow found time for everyone. Her love was her ministry—it showed in how she mothered, how she gave, and how she lived.

As a mother, she was unmatched. She wasn't just a parent to her own children; she was a mother figure to many. Her nieces, nephews, and even neighborhood kids knew her as someone who would go above and beyond. She had a heart that stretched far beyond the walls of her own home. No child was a stranger to her—she gave hugs, guidance, and the kind of love that lingered long after she left the room.

Even when life tested her, she rose above it. She faced storms, but she didn't let them define her. Her strength came from within—a kind of quiet resilience that kept her moving forward. There was something powerful about how she carried herself, how she smiled through struggles, and how she believed that every setback was just a setup for a comeback.

Those who knew her best say she had a gift for lifting others, even when she needed lifting herself. Her smile could change a mood, her laughter could shift a room, and her spirit could make anyone believe in hope again.

Shendora "Rose" Black was a mama, a dreamer, and a fighter. Her life reminds us that no matter what life throws your way, you can keep rising, keep loving, and keep building. She was more than a name—she was a light. And though her journey ended too soon, her legacy continues to shine through everyone who loved her.

THE PAIN BEHIND THE SMILE

While she showed up for everyone else, behind closed doors, Shendora was in a relationship that slowly tried to dim her light. What many didn't see—or didn't fully understand—was the emotional and controlling abuse she endured.

Her partner was jealous, manipulative, and possessive. He kept her isolated from family. He didn't want visitors. He didn't like her male cousins. His behavior was filled with control masked as concern. It's a reminder that abuse isn't always loud or visible—sometimes, it hides behind forced smiles and unanswered texts.

What looked like "just staying home" was actually isolation. What seemed like "she's not answering her phone" was really fear and silence. He monitored who came around, questioned her about where she went, and made it difficult for her to feel safe, even among loved ones. Little by little, he cut off her lifelines—the very people who could've helped her escape sooner.

Yet even through that, she kept smiling. Kept loving. Kept giving. That was who she was. And that's the part that breaks hearts the most—because even while she was fighting her own battles, she kept showing up for everyone else.

Today, her family is still picking up the pieces. The weight of this loss is heavy. Her children are grieving. Her parents and siblings are still waking up to the reality that she's not coming back. The smile they once saw every day is now a memory. But through that pain, they press on—with strength she instilled in them.

There's an empty seat at the table now. A silence in places where her laugh once rang. Her absence is loud. But her love is louder. The way she lived, gave, and loved left a lasting imprint on every heart she touched.

Her family continues to share her story—not just to remember her—but to help others recognize the signs. They speak her name so other women (and men) can find the courage to walk away. Her story is now a lifeline for someone else. A warning. A whisper in the dark saying, "You don't have to stay. You can leave. You can live."

Domestic violence doesn't always look like bruises. Sometimes it looks like a beautiful woman showing up for others while silently hoping someone shows up for her. It looks like missed family gatherings, changed phone numbers, and long pauses before answering, "Are you okay?"

This page of Shendora's story isn't easy to read, but it's necessary. Because awareness saves lives. Because silence can kill. And because no one should have to fight for their life in the name of love.

Let this page be a mirror and a megaphone. Let her story remind us to check on our strong friends, the ones who always say "I'm fine." Let it stir us to ask deeper questions, pay closer attention, and create safe spaces for those silently suffering.

Her pain may have been hidden, but her legacy won't be.

HER STORY WILL SAVE SOMEONE

This fall, as we observe Domestic Violence Awareness Month, we honor Shendora not just as a victim—but as a light, a mother, a dreamer, and a woman who deserved more time.

Her legacy reminds us that it's never too early to walk away—but it can be too late. That abuse doesn't only happen to women. That control is not love. And that your peace really is everything.

If Shendora could speak to other women right now, her message would be clear:

"Run. Don't stay where you're constantly being broken. You are too beautiful to keep putting yourself in places that hurt. Find your peace. Live for you. Live for your babies."

We will remember her every October. We will say her name. We will tell her story so another woman finds the courage to leave before it's too late.

Because her life mattered.
And her peace was everything.

BUBBLY. BOLD. BEAUTIFUL. BELOVED.

Shendora Black, affectionately known as Rose, was a radiant light in every space she entered. Born and raised in Bainbridge, Georgia, she was known for her warm smile, her infectious laugh, and a presence that lit up the room before she even spoke. A true Southern soul, she brought joy, comfort, and strength to her family, her children, and her community.

Rose was the kind of woman who made strangers feel like family and always showed up when someone needed her most. A devoted mother, a loyal daughter, and a deeply loving aunt, she lived to nurture and uplift others. No child was a stranger to her—she mothered with intention, loved without limits, and created safe spaces wherever she went.

She had big dreams—especially the vision to own her own trucking company, a legacy she was building with love and patience. Every move she made was for her children, her future, and her peace.

SHENDORA
Rose Black

Shendora's journey was filled with triumphs and trials, but even in the face of adversity, she held her head high. Her strength was quiet but undeniable. Though her life was cut short due to domestic violence, her story continues to shine a light on what it means to be a fighter, a giver, and a woman of purpose.

In her own words:

"Your peace is everything. Find that, and live for you and your babies."

Her life mattered. Her story speaks. Her legacy lives on.

www.lashawndashiree.info/domestic-survivor-s-testimony

Recognizing survivors: October is Domestic Survivor Awareness Month

MAHALIA GRIER
Staff Reporter

October is Domestic Violence Awareness Month. It's a time to honor victims and survivors who were mentally and physically abused by their partners. Lashawnda Shiree Love is a survivor of domestic violence. Love was born in Bainbridge, and has a career, a husband, and three children, but she has a grim past that she's willing to share with others. From 2011 to 2012, Love had an affair with a married man while she was also married. Eventually, both decided to divorce their spouses and get married to each other. Love heard rumors that the man was abusive to another young lady he was married to previously, but Love admitted that

"He was fine, and he was nice. So, I didn't get any of the vibes that he was abusive because he was really kind." After Love was married, she stated everything was beautiful,

"Everything was beautiful to me because I was in a previous marriage, and I was really depressed, overweight, and sad. I just wasn't happy. So, he made me feel happy. Everything to me was blissful; I just had the best time of my life." She continued, "I thought he was the best person because he was a pastor, but when I got pregnant things kind of shifted."

Love explains that constant arguments were happening in the relationship, and the tension escalated when she chose to not attend family events due to certain situations. This decision marked the beginning of the abuse. The incidents typically occurred when her two sons from her previous marriage were away for the weekend with their father. When her sons returned, they noticed signs of violence in the home, like patched-up holes in the walls and regular glass windows replaced with fiberglass so the windows wouldn't shatter explosively.

From 2013 to 2018, Love didn't disclose any information about her abuse to anyone because she stated, "He was a pastor. He was a prophet, and I didn't want him to be embarrassed nor did I want people to say 'That's what you get. We were just waiting for him to beat her up,' and I don't want people to feel joy out of knowing I'm going through this."

In 2018, Love experienced a nervous breakdown when the man began an affair with someone close to her. This betrayal worsened the abuse, as the individual shared personal details about Love that she hadn't disclosed to him. "She revealed things I had kept private, which triggered even more violent behavior from him." Eventually, the man left Love for this person.

In 2018, after enduring ongoing abuse, Love confided in her family and declared she would not return to the man, but eventually, she did. After his apology, they reconciled, but in 2019, the situation escalated when he attempted to take her life.

A day before Thanksgiving in 2019, Love received a phone call informing her that the man had purchased a trailer with his girlfriend. Initially doubtful, she later confirmed it by searching online and uncovering two and a half years of location history that revealed the man had been lying about where he had been. This discovery led Love to realize just how little she truly knew about him. "I didn't know anything about him. He's from Florida, and I'm from Bainbridge. It seemed like during our courtship, he was getting to know me, but in reality, he was gathering information on me," she reflected. "He never shared much about himself, and if he did, he was vague and never fully honest. For instance, he would say, 'I'm going to the store', but omit that the store was in Jacksonville." Despite this, Love still didn't leave.

Later, Love took him for throat surgery. During this period, Love became more suspicious of his actions. While they were filming a Facebook Live video called "Transformation Tuesday," she installed a tracking app on his phone–the only time she had access to it. When she tried to access his information while he was in surgery, she discovered he had changed his password. Soon after, when they returned home, the police arrived with paperwork accusing Love of harassment and stalking, based on claims made by the man's girlfriend, which intensified their conflict. It was during this time that the abuse nearly ended her life.

At the beginning of May 2020, Love had a dream that left her confused about its meaning. It was not until later that month, on May 24, when she unexpectedly received divorce papers in the mail. Love stated the message from God became clear. She said God instructed her to take the dream to a woman she knew who didn't know anything about her situation. The woman, unaware of Love's situation, delivered a powerful message: "If you go back this time, you're going to die." That warning ended Love's relationship with the man, though she hadn't realized that he had already filed for divorce earlier in the month. After receiving the paperwork, Love stopped speaking to the man, and for the next two years, they did not exchange words. Reflecting on that time, she shared, "It took two years to have words whenever we were in each other's presence. I was still hurt. I was still upset. I couldn't form anything into words." Following the divorce, Love briefly dated but quickly shifted her focus to her children. She often spoke to the Lord about the abuse she endured and carried guilt for a long time. "I felt guilty because I believed this was what I deserved for what I did. I stayed as long as I did because I thought it was my punishment for taking another woman's husband," she said. But she stated God revealed to her that, despite her mistakes, "He didn't have the right to abuse me the way that he did." She said God sent her a husband, David Hassan Habbi Love, to find her, and today she is happy and whole.

Love wants to inform women and men before they are in a relationship "to know the red flags when you see them. Find safe people that you can trust. I told my family, but they weren't safe people because they used it against me. You need a safe person who's not going to judge you, and if you've never been in this situation before then you can't judge it."

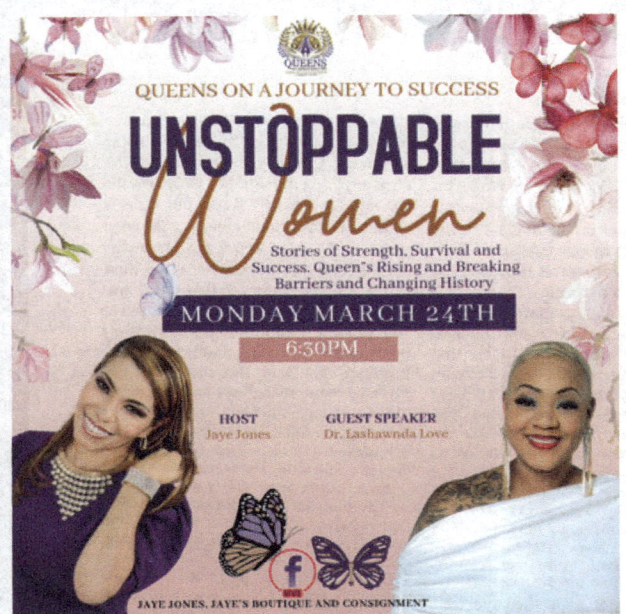

RECOGNIZING SURVIVORS:

DOMESTIC VIOLENCE AWARENESS MONTH

By Dr. Lashawnda Love

October is Domestic Violence Month. It's a time to honor victims and survivors who were mentally and physically abused by their partners. Lashawnda Shiree Love is a victim and survivor of domestic violence. Love was born in Bainbridge, and she has a career, a husband, and three children. She has a grim past that she's willing to share with others.

From 2011-2012, Love had an affair with a married man while she was also married. Eventually, both decided to divorce their spouses and get married to each other. Love heard rumors that the man was abusive to another young lady he was married to previously, but Love admitted that, "He was fine, and he was nice. So, I didn't get any of the vibes that he was abusive because he was really kind." After Love was married, she exclaimed everything was beautiful, "Everything was beautiful to me because I was in a previous marriage, and I was really depressed, overweight, and sad. I just wasn't happy. So, he made me feel happy. Everything to me was blissful; I just had the best time of my life." She continued, "I thought he was the best person because he was a pastor, but when I got pregnant, things kind of shifted.

Love explains that constant arguments were happening in the relationship, and the tension escalated when she chose not to attend family events due to certain situations. This decision marked the beginning of the abuse. The incidents typically occurred when her two sons from her previous marriage were away for the weekend with their father. When her sons returned, they noticed signs of violence in the home, like patched-up holes in the walls and fiberglass windows, which had been replaced because regular glass would shatter explosively.

BOOK RELEASE
WHEN CHOICES HURT
A JOURNEY OF REDEMPTION FROM DOMESTIC VIOLENCE

For years, I carried the weight of pain, betrayal, and anger. But today, I stand here healed and free, no longer bound by the chains of bitterness. My journey through the darkness of domestic violence wasn't easy, but it was necessary for my growth, healing, and redemption.

I wrote When Choices Hurt: A Journey of Redemption from Domestic Violence to share my story, offer hope, and remind every woman in a similar situation that healing is possible.

If you or someone you love is struggling, this book is for you. There is freedom on the other side of abuse.

AUTHOR
Dr. Lashawnda Love

AVAILABLE ON AMAZON — GET YOUR COPY TODAY!

From 2013-2018, Love didn't disclose any information about her abuse to anyone because she stated, "He was a pastor. He was a prophet, and I didn't want him to be embarrassed, nor did I want people to say, 'that's what you get. We were just waiting for him to beat her up', and I don't want people to feel joy out of knowing I'm going through this."

In 2018, Love experienced a nervous breakdown when the man began an affair with someone close to her. This betrayal worsened the abuse, as the individual shared personal details about Love that she hadn't disclosed to him. "She revealed things I had kept private, which triggered even more violent behavior from him." Eventually, the man left Love for this person.

In 2018, Love experienced a nervous breakdown when the man began an affair with someone close to her. This betrayal worsened the abuse, as the individual shared personal details about Love that she hadn't disclosed to him. "She revealed things I had kept private, which triggered even more violent behavior from him." Eventually, the man left Love for this person.

.In 2018, after enduring ongoing abuse, Love confided in her family and declared she would not return to the man, but eventually, she did. After his apology, they reconciled, but in 2019, the situation escalated when he attempted to take her life. Afterwards, Love informed her family of her abuse, and she stated that she would not go back to him and filed for divorce, but the man apologized and Love went back with him and ended the divorce in 2019.

From then on, the man was not allowed at the house because Love's two sons and nephew lived with her, and her sons threatened the man. Love saw the man Monday through Friday in Midway at the Ministry because that's where she worked.

A day before Thanksgiving in 2019, Love received a phone call informing her that the man had purchased a trailer with his girlfriend. Initially doubtful, she later confirmed it by searching online and uncovering two and a half years of location history that revealed the man had been lying about where he had been. This discovery led Love to realize just how little she truly knew about him. "I didn't know anything about him.

Later, Love took him for throat surgery. During this period, Love became more suspicious of his actions. While they were filming a Facebook Live video called "Transformation Tuesday," she installed a tracking app on his phone—the only time she had access to it. When she tried to access his information while he was in surgery, she discovered he had changed his password. Soon after, when they returned home, the police arrived with paperwork accusing Love of harassment and stalking, based on claims made by the man's girlfriend, which intensified their conflict. It was during this time that the abuse nearly ended her life.

WHEN CHOICES HURT

A JOURNEY REDEMPTION
DOMESTIC VIOLENCE

At the beginning of May 2020, Love had a dream that left her confused about its meaning. It wasn't until later that month, on May 24, when she unexpectedly received divorce papers in the mail, that the message from God became clear. God instructed her to take the dream to a woman she knew who didn't know anything about her situation. The woman, unaware of Love's situation, delivered a powerful message: "If you go back this time, you're going to die." That warning ended Love's relationship with the man, though she hadn't realized that he had already filed for divorce earlier in the month. After receiving the paperwork, Love stopped speaking to the man, and for the next two years, they did not exchange words. Reflecting on that time, she shared, "It took two years to have words whenever we were in each other's presence. I was still hurt. I was still upset. I couldn't form anything into words." Following the divorce, Love briefly dated but quickly shifted her focus to her children. She often spoke to the Lord about the abuse she endured and carried guilt for a long time. "I felt guilty because I believed this was what I deserved for what I did. I stayed as long as I did because I thought it was my punishment for taking another woman's husband," she said. But God revealed to her that, despite her mistakes, "He didn't have the right to abuse me the way that he did." God then sent her husband David Hassan Habbi Love to find her, and today she is happy and whole.

Dr. Wallace C. Cooper Jr.: The Bridge Between Revelation and Reality

By Dr. Lashawnda Love, Stork Publishing LLC

Dr. Wallace C. Cooper Jr. is not just a man of the cloth—he's a man of deep clarity, creative courage, and cultural confrontation. With over 30 years in ministry, he has emerged as a trusted apostolic voice in spaces where silence once ruled. His work dismantles comfort zones, inviting his audience—whether in pews or on pages—into the raw, redemptive process of truth.

What sets Dr. Cooper apart is his ability to bridge the sacred and the personal without compromise. His sermons pierce. His writings unravel. His mentorship transforms. But none of it is performative. It is purpose-driven. Every message is born from lived experience, every book chapter shaped by spiritual warfare and personal testimony.

As a seasoned pastor and Chief Overseer of God Way Apostolic Faith International Ministries, he leads with conviction, but without condemnation. His leadership is anchored in accountability, his influence fortified by transparency.

Whether he's exposing hidden truths in The Life of a DL Preacher, diving into emotional and spiritual tension in Why Love, or exploring divine timing and transformation in Dynamic of Impact, Dr. Cooper uses storytelling as strategy. His words are both mirror and map—calling readers to confront themselves, then guiding them toward breakthrough.

In a time where performance often overshadows power, Dr. Wallace C. Cooper Jr. remains rooted in truth, committed to growth, and unapologetically called.

MEET MADUKE
THE SOUL OF THE STORY, THE FIRE OF THE FAMILY

By Stork Publishing LLC, Dr. Lashawnda Love

In a world that often masks pain with performance, MaDuke shines as a beacon of authenticity, laughter, and unwavering wisdom. As the heart and humor behind the legacy of Dr. Wallace C. Cooper Jr., MaDuke is more than just a personality—she's a movement.

With a voice that commands attention and a presence that instantly disarms, MaDuke has become the glue of her family and a voice of encouragement in the community. Whether she's speaking at events, delivering unforgettable one-liners, or simply showing up with that signature joy, MaDuke embodies what it means to lead with love and stand strong in truth.

She's not the kind of woman who walks in quietly. She walks in with purpose—and brings peace with her.

A Legacy of Laughter and Leadership
MaDuke has mastered the art of making people feel seen. Known for her quick wit and tough-love guidance, she has a way of transforming chaos into clarity. Her humor is disarming, but it's her wisdom and discernment that leave a lasting impact.

At home, she is the calm during storms and the light when things feel dim. She knows how to bring a family together—whether it's through a meal, a prayer, or a much-needed moment of truth. MaDuke doesn't just talk unity; she lives it.

Outside the home, she's a sought-after motivator—bringing her no-nonsense, real-life approach to stages and conversations. She reminds everyone that life is hard, but quitting is not an option. Her messages are rooted in lived experience, fueled by faith, and anchored in compassion.

"I don't sugarcoat the truth—because healing don't happen in silence." – MaDuke

WHEN WISDOM MEETS BOLDNESS

While MaDuke commands attention in her own right, she shares the spotlight with a powerhouse: Dr. Wallace C. Cooper Jr. Together, they form a partnership defined by balance—his deep introspection and prophetic storytelling paired with her clarity, warmth, and insight.

Dr. Cooper has carved a space for bold, soul-searching literature that challenges, confronts, and convicts. His growing catalog of work includes:

- The Life of a DL Preacher
- Why Love
- Die, Live, Hate, Love, Cry, Laugh
- Naughty and Nice
- Dynamic of Impact
- Let's Deal with it Raw and Uncut

Each title is a window into the human experience—tackling secrecy, identity, intimacy, faith, and emotional resilience. His latest work, Let's Deal with it Raw and Uncut, continues the theme of honesty that defines his ministry and writing.

What sets his voice apart is his willingness to tell the truth—the kind of truth that heals, challenges, and exposes what most would prefer to keep hidden.

Two Forces, One Purpose

Together, MaDuke and Dr. Cooper are more than a couple—they are a dynamic mission. She steadies the foundation while he pushes the envelope. She softens the blows with humor and heart while he delivers the unfiltered truth through pen and pulpit.

Their synergy has birthed not just books and messages, but movements. From community initiatives to ministry outreach and creative ventures like Cooper's (MaDuke Tha Deva) Entertainment Production LLC, the impact of their work is evident both locally and beyond.

MaDuke remains central to it all. Her influence is quiet in some rooms and resounding in others, but always essential. She has the rare ability to keep things real without tearing things down—an anointing many strive for but few truly possess.

WHY THE WORLD NEEDS MADUKE

> **"You can laugh your way through pain if you let faith lead the punchline."** – MaDuke

In every community, there's someone you look to when life gets heavy. Someone who will tell it to you straight, but still hold your hand while you cry. That's who MaDuke is.

She is a woman of laughter, but also of legacy. She doesn't just help people feel better—she helps them be better. Her authenticity is refreshing. Her faith is unwavering. And her example is proof that you can lead with both truth and tenderness.

For those who have the privilege of knowing her, MaDuke is unforgettable. And for those yet to meet her, one conversation will show you why she's not just the fire of the family—she's the force holding it all together.

She reminds us that:
- You can laugh and lead at the same time
- You can correct and cover with the same voice
- You can be strong and soft without apology

This Summer, as B.A.B.Y. Magazine shines the spotlight on voices of legacy and authenticity, MaDuke takes center stage—not for fame, but for the powerful example she continues to set every day.

LITERARY LIBRARY

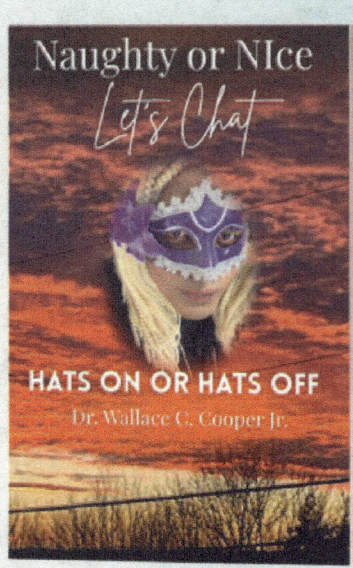
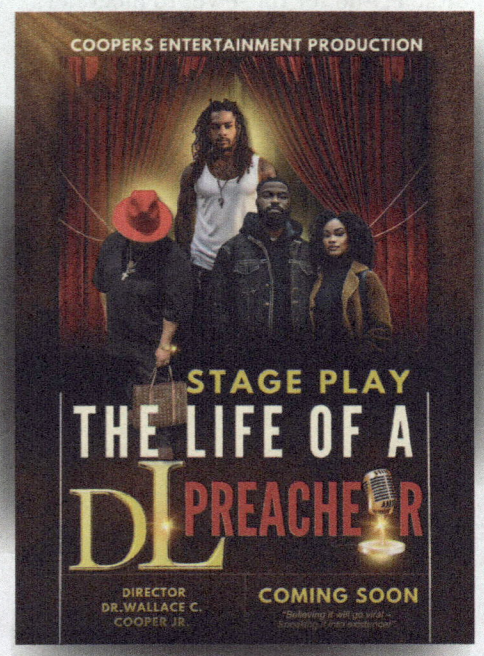

"I may not have all the answers, but I know how to hold people together when everything's falling apart."

LEGACY UNFILTERED: A FINAL WORD

Dr. Wallace C. Cooper Jr. stands as a living reminder that truth, when spoken boldly and lived authentically, has the power to heal generations. From the pulpit to the page, and from the private struggles to the public call, his life is a blueprint for leadership rooted in transparency. Alongside the wisdom and heart of MaDuke, their legacy is one of honesty, hope, and healing. They are proof that ministry isn't confined to Sunday mornings—it's found in how you live, love, lead, and tell the truth. As this Summer 2025 edition of B.A.B.Y. Magazine closes, we leave you with one thought: When God trusts someone with truth, He also trusts them with people. And that's exactly what Dr. Cooper and MaDuke carry—people, purpose, and power.

May their story inspire you to live yours with the same boldness.

BORN TO LEAD
THE POWER, PURPOSE & RESILIENCE OF
Keiaundria Ragland

In a world that often tells women to shrink, Keiaundria Ragland chose to rise. As the visionary behind She's PurposeKe, a thriving movement and brand built to lead, serve, and elevate women of faith, Keiaundria's journey is nothing short of divine resilience.

Born and raised in Knoxville, Tennessee, Keiaundria's life story isn't about perfection—it's about purpose. She openly shares that her journey to confidence, calling, and coaching began in the quiet place of journaling during a season of deep reflection. It was in those pages, surrounded by self-doubt and a longing to understand her worth, that God began to reveal something greater. What started as personal healing transformed into her first self-published book, Life at a Glance: Single, Married, Togetherness, released in 2018.

BUT KEIAUNDRIA DIDN'T STOP THERE.

She went on to co-author her first anthology chapter, Seeking the Father Figure "IN HIM", in 2019, and now proudly contributes to Born to Lead: Awaken the Leader Within, where she tells a deeper story—one of resilience, trust, and bold leadership. "Trust the process," she says. "Leading others caused me to become intentional about my life, my career, and my business."

As the CEO of She's PurposeKe, she now coaches Christian professional women who feel stuck. Through her signature programs like From Stress to Success and Reignite Your Passion, she helps women identify limiting beliefs, reclaim their God-given power, and move from burnout to breakthrough.

Her reach stretches far beyond coaching. Keiaundria is an author, speaker, podcast guest, radio personality, TV broadcaster, and event specialist. She's graced stages and platforms like Hope-In-Christ Podcast, Be Inspired with Ursula, and Kingdom Purpose TV, and her work has been featured in Women's Enterprise Magazine, FREE2BME Magazine, and numerous conferences, including the I Am H.E.R International Awards.

> "GOD DIDN'T JUST CALL ME TO SURVIVE—HE CALLED ME TO LEAD, TO EMPOWER, AND TO SHOW WOMEN THAT HEALING AND PURPOSE CAN WALK HAND IN HAND."
> – KEIAUNDRIA RAGLAND

Through it all, she credits God for every open door. "Everything concerning me, the Lord perfected," she shares, standing firm on Psalm 138:8—"The Lord will vindicate me; your love, Lord, endures forever – do not abandon the works of your hands."

Her aunt Helen's story continues to inspire her—reminding her, and now others, not to let the world's "no" keep them from their divine assignment.

Keiaundria's legacy is clear: She was born to lead. And now, she awakens the leader in others—one prayer, one session, one book at a time.

> "DON'T DISMISS YOUR SMALL BEGINNINGS. GOD IS USING EVERY STEP TO SHAPE THE LEADER YOU WERE BORN TO BE."
> – KEIAUNDRIA RAGLAND

Photo Credit: Michelle Zelina-Stice
Learn more: www.shespurposeke.com
Contact: lifeataglancebooks@gmail.com | 865-382-2761
Social: Facebook, Twitter, Instagram @shespurposeke |
LinkedIn: Keiaundria Ragland

PORSHA & JOSHUA Hunt

FROM BROKEN TO BLESSED:
Porsha Hunt's
TESTIMONY OF UNRELENTING LOVE AND UNSTOPPABLE GRACE

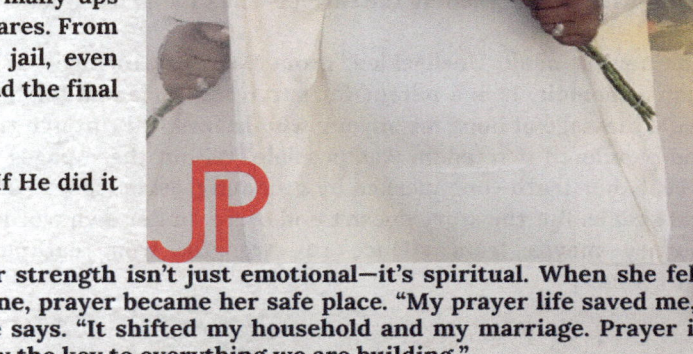

When people talk about fairy-tale marriages, they often leave out the parts that require real faith, deep forgiveness, and raw endurance. But for Porsha Hunt, marriage has been just that—a walk of transformation, not perfection. Since saying "I do" to Joshul D. Hunt in 2013, she has weathered storms that would've drowned others, but today she stands healed, whole, and happily married.

Their love story has not been without hardship. "We've had many ups and downs, smiles and frowns, good days and bad days," she shares. From infidelity, deception, and years of him being in and out of jail, even selling drugs—the enemy tried to tear them apart, but grace had the final say.

Through it all, Porsha says, "God has shifted both of our lives. If He did it for us, He will do it for you."

Her strength isn't just emotional—it's spiritual. When she felt alone, prayer became her safe place. "My prayer life saved me," she says. "It shifted my household and my marriage. Prayer is now the key to everything we are building."

The scripture that anchored her through the hardest moments?
1 Corinthians 13:5 – Love keeps no record of wrongs.
"I wanted to walk away so many times," she admits, "but this verse taught me how to love in spite of the pain. Not blindly, but biblically—with grace, not grudges."

Her advice to other women walking through betrayal or brokenness is simple but profound:
"Matthew 6:33. Seek first the kingdom of God and His righteousness—and He'll add everything else. No matter what you go through, GROW through it. Seek God and watch Him add His glory to your story."

And Porsha's story doesn't end with survival—it's about legacy. "I may have been broken," she declares, "but now I am healed, whole, complete, grateful, and thankful. God has kept me. He never left me. So don't you dare give up on love, because God didn't give up on you."

As a woman married in ministry, Porsha knows how important spiritual unity is—but she also knows how to honor the journey when your spouse is still growing.
"Before my husband got locked up, he would come to church sometimes. But now he has a personal relationship with God, and I'm so grateful." Even when he didn't attend, he always supported her calling. "The biggest lesson I've learned is to meet people where they are. I never made him feel low—I made sure he always felt loved."

Now, as they prepare to attend church together when he returns home this year, Porsha sees the promise fulfilled:
Redemption is real. Restoration is possible. And love—true, God-centered love—is worth the fight.

UNSHACKLED

FROM DARKNESS TO LIGHT – THE BOLD TESTIMONY OF

Evangelist Atiya Jenkins

From the streets of Atlantic City to the sacred places of ministry and healing, Evangelist Atiya Jenkins is a walking testimony of God's power to redeem, restore, and rebuild. As a proud mother of two sons and a spiritual leader with a heart on fire for outreach, Atiya is not just preaching the Gospel—she's living it out loud.

Her newest book, Unshackled: From Darkness to Light, is more than a memoir. It is a mirror for survivors, a manual for healing, and a message of hope for anyone who has walked through trauma and wondered if freedom was possible. Within these pages, Atiya reveals her truth—one marked by grooming, sexual abuse, silence, and shame. But the story doesn't end there. In her own words, this journey moves from silence to strength, from darkness to deliverance.

"CHAINS FELL OFF: THE HEALING MISSION OF EVANGELIST ATIYA JENKINS"

Since her salvation in 2007, Atiya has been driven by an unshakable call to serve the broken, the overlooked, and the abandoned. "I wrote this book not just for myself, but for the woman who still cries in silence, for the man who thinks healing isn't for him, and for the child within us who still needs to hear, 'You are not alone.'" Her voice, once stifled by pain, now rings with clarity and conviction.

As a certified life coach, counselor, author, and spiritual midwife, Atiya's ministry focuses on walking with others through transformation. Whether through her writing, her workshops, or one-on-one coaching, she equips people to confront their past and break free from the shame that has held them hostage for too long. "Healing begins with truth," she says. "And the truth is—your past does not cancel your purpose."

"HER VOICE RETURNED: A SURVIVOR'S CALL TO THE BROKEN AND BRAVE"

Her passion reaches far beyond individual transformation. Atiya is dedicated to restoring families, strengthening communities, and encouraging ministry beyond the church walls. Her outreach work has become the heartbeat of her calling, bringing light to places often left in the shadows.

When asked why she chose the title Unshackled, Atiya explains, "Because that's what healing feels like. Like the chains are finally falling off. Like you're finally free to breathe, to speak, to live."

Atiya Jenkins has turned her pain into power and her story into a safe place for others to heal. Her mission is clear—to awaken the light in others and lead them to the God who heals deeply, completely, and forever.

If you've ever wondered if your voice matters or if your story is too broken to be used—let this book be your answer. You are not too far gone. You are not forgotten. You are unshackled.

Dr. Melissa V. Leon:
TAKING THE GOSPEL
ON THE ROAD AND INTO HEARTS

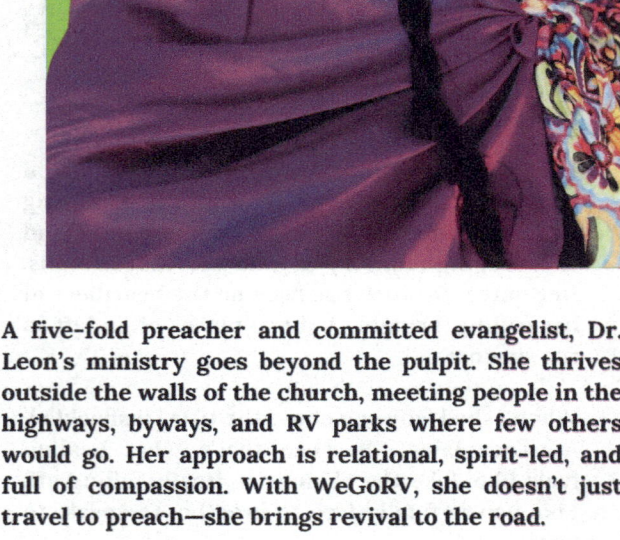

Bold, anointed, and full of grace, Dr. Melissa V. Leon is a woman on divine assignment. As the Founder and Senior Leader of Worldwide Evangelism Gospel Outreach RV Ministry (WeGoRV), she travels far and wide—proclaiming the gospel, empowering believers, and calling the lost to Christ. Whether she's preaching on the road, writing, singing, or styling someone into confidence, Dr. Leon's life is a living epistle of God's power, beauty, and love.

Affectionately known as "GiGi", this Florida native from St. Petersburg balances many roles: mother, grandmother, chaplain, minister, singer, poet, and revivalist. Her most recent release, the inspirational poetry book "Joy Jewels", is a deeply personal reflection of her faith journey—filled with grace, strength, and encouragement for every reader.

A five-fold preacher and committed evangelist, Dr. Leon's ministry goes beyond the pulpit. She thrives outside the walls of the church, meeting people in the highways, byways, and RV parks where few others would go. Her approach is relational, spirit-led, and full of compassion. With WeGoRV, she doesn't just travel to preach—she brings revival to the road.

Her voice also reaches the masses through her weekly podcast, "Transparency Time with GiGi," where she confronts real-life issues with truth and tenderness. It's a space where shame dies, healing begins, and the gospel is unapologetically applied.

A five-fold preacher and committed evangelist, Dr. Leon's ministry goes beyond the pulpit. She thrives outside the walls of the church, meeting people in the highways, byways, and RV parks where few others would go. Her approach is relational, spirit-led, and full of compassion. With WeGoRV, she doesn't just travel to preach—she brings revival to the road.

Her voice also reaches the masses through her weekly podcast, "Transparency Time with GiGi," where she confronts real-life issues with truth and tenderness. It's a space where shame dies, healing begins, and the gospel is unapologetically applied.

ATTENTION
FREE SERVICE

Do you need your Bio Rewritten? Well Stork Publishing LLC will rewrite yours for free!

A WOMAN OF CHARACTER AND *Integrity*

BY DR. YAQUANDA PAYNE-MCCALL

Dr. YaQuanda Payne-McCall is a woman of character and integrity. Her testimony is proof that Christ can ensure you don't look like what you've been through! Having been delivered from fornication, cursing, lying, clubbing, stealing, the guilt of abortions, marijuana abuse, alcohol abuse, and a host of other sins, Dr. McCall deeply appreciates the loving grace of God. After enduring abuse as a child and mistreatment as a teenager, YaQuanda overcame her past by the power of Christ.

YaQuanda was well acquainted with fear, doubt, self-hate, pride, suicide attempts, drug dealers, thugs, killers, womanizers, prostitutes, homosexuals, mental battles, depression, and many other struggles. Her testimony demonstrates how the heart of God, coupled with His power, can destroy yokes in the lives of all she encounters! Dr. McCall firmly believes: "My past does not dictate my destiny!" Her no-nonsense approach to mediocrity is a commanding force behind her vision. YaQuanda is a compassionate, loving, and warm woman of God who seeks to please the Father.

Dr. YaQuanda is filled with the Holy Ghost, with signs and wonders following her ministry. She has four adult children (Arielle, Arionne, Tommy Elisha, and Timothy Elijah), who have served alongside her in ministry in various capacities. She is the daughter of Fred Payne and Dr. Vanessa Williams.

Dr. YaQuanda is the Founder and President of I Speak Life Global Ministries, Inc. She is also the lead intercessor of the 5am Prayer SHiFT broadcast, where she and her team have prayed every morning on Facebook LIVE for over seven years and counting.

Dr. YaQuanda hosts three conferences annually. For seven years, she has hosted the For Men Only SHiFT Conference, where men gather to be encouraged and empowered through the Word of God, praise and worship, testimonies, fellowship, prophecy, deliverance, and prayer.

She also hosts the sheSHiFT Women's Conference, which empowers and educates women through the Word of God with various speakers imparting wisdom on topics essential to women. Additionally, the SHiFT Therapy SupernaturalSummit highlights the importance of mental health and suicide awareness. As a marriage and family counselor, Dr. Q understands the value of educating family members and friends to recognize the signs of mental illness and suicidal behavior.

This summit includes panels, workshops, classes, worship services, individual and family sessions, and community awareness programs.

Dr. McCall prays with and for hundreds of people daily, virtually. She offers classes to help others grow in their prayer lives and their relationship with the Lord. She has led countless sinners and backsliders back to God.

relationship with the Lord. She has led countless sinners and backsliders back to God.

She is a licensed, ordained, and confirmed minister of the Gospel, having served as an Associate Pastor. Dr. YaQuanda hosts SHiFT Conversations both virtually and in person. These conversations have been a lifeline for many, as God uses these testimonies to help others overcome.

Dr. YaQuanda travels internationally, preaching the Good News of Jesus Christ. With her passport ready, Dr. McCall continues to travel around the world, preaching the Word of God and allowing Him to use her however He sees fit. Dr. McCall casts out devils, speaks life, and lays hands on the sick, and they recover. She has prayed for countless people both in person and virtually, witnessing the power of God defeat every evil force.

Dr. McCall walks in the authority and power of God, operating in an undeniable degree of glory that commands change in others. YaQuanda is known for teaching and preaching with simplicity and revelatory power. She has faithfully served on the Pastoral Staff and as a Marriage Ministry leader at TGDC in Tallahassee, Florida, under the leadership of Pastor Joseph Davis for over 13 years. Dr. McCall has received numerous awards and honors, including the Resilience Award for her commitment to prayer and daily encouragement of God's people.

Dr. YaQuanda Payne-McCall is the author of Successful Marriage: God's Way, along with several other books and workbooks. Dr. McCall is also a recording artist who travels and ministers in song with her daughters. She has served as a college professor, seminar instructor, seminar facilitator, speaker, preacher, teacher, worship leader, songwriter, and more. The Father has graciously bestowed many talents upon her. Dr. McCall is also a sought-after keynote speaker at Women's Conferences, Prophetic Conferences, Empowerment Summits, Business Seminars, Men's Conferences, and much more.

Dr. McCall graduated from Florida A&M University with a Bachelor's degree in Computer Information Systems. She also holds a Master's degree in Christian Counseling from Jacksonville Theological Seminary. Additionally, YaQuanda earned her Doctorate in Christian Education from Truth Bible College and Seminary. She has completed the School of the Prophets, the School of the Prophetic, and the School of Prayer. Dr. McCall is a devoted student of the Word, endeavoring to teach others about the Way, the Truth, and the Life.

A Journey to Healing and Hope
The Mission Behind Queens on a Journey to Success

JERMERICA JONES

Every journey of healing begins with a single step—a step away from pain, trauma, and adversity, toward strength, resilience, and hope. For many women, including myself, this step comes after enduring experiences that leave deep scars but also ignite a fire within us to rise, rebuild, and reach out to others who are still walking through their own dark valleys.

My name is Jermerica Jones, and I am the founder of Queens on a Journey to Success, a movement born from my personal story of overcoming trauma, including molestation, rape, domestic violence, and challenges with incarceration. My mission is to create a space where women, whether their experiences involve similar hardships or different forms of adversity, can find support, empowerment, and practical resources to transform their lives.

Healing Through Community

One of the core principles behind Queens on a Journey to Success is that no woman should have to navigate her struggles alone. When women who have endured trauma—whether it be sexual assault, domestic violence, or the isolating effects of incarceration—come together, something remarkable happens. A sense of community forms, creating a powerful force for healing and growth.

At Queens on a Journey to Success, we believe in helping women rebuild every aspect of their lives. Through mentorship, education, and emotional support, we provide the tools they need not only to survive but to thrive in all areas of their lives. Our goal is to give them the opportunity to rewrite their stories and become the queens they were always meant to be.

Empowering Women to Reclaim Their Lives

Every queen has a journey, and each journey is unique. For many of the women I work with, the road to success has been paved with unimaginable struggles. Whether it's rebuilding after an abusive relationship, finding employment after incarceration, or healing from years of emotional wounds, we focus on equipping women with the skills, resources, and confidence needed to achieve success.

Our programs help them find jobs, provide educational opportunities, and offer counseling to support emotional healing. We also connect them with safe havens, ensuring they have both physical and emotional spaces to recover and rebuild. Most importantly, we ensure that every woman leaves our program empowered, with a renewed sense of purpose and equipped with the tools to navigate the next steps of her life.

Breaking the Silence

Breaking the silence is another pillar of Queens on a Journey to Success. We are dedicated to raising awareness and breaking the silence surrounding domestic violence, sexual assault, and incarceration. Too often, women in these situations remain silent due to shame, fear, or societal stigma. But their voices are powerful, and their stories are important.

Through events, workshops, and public speaking engagements, I aim to shatter the silence and amplify the voices of women who have experienced these traumas. By sharing my own story, I hope to inspire others to speak up, seek help, and know that they are not alone. I want to encourage women to see that there is life after trauma, that healing is possible, and that success is within reach, no matter how difficult the past has been.

Hope and Future

The mission of Queens on a Journey to Success is ultimately about hope. It's about showing women that no matter where they've been or what they've gone through, there is always hope for a brighter future. It's about lifting them up, providing them with the tools and support they need, and walking with them on their journey to success.

As I continue to expand this mission, I am committed to ensuring that every woman we serve leaves feeling empowered, uplifted, and prepared to take the next steps in her journey. Together, we are queens rising above our past, ready to embrace a future filled with healing, hope, and success.

MEET YOUR
Life Coach

For over 11 years, I've proudly served as a certified life coach, empowering individuals and teams to unlock their potential and achieve meaningfully results. As a multi-talented individual, I wear many hats, including being a business owner, minister, community service provider, author, ghostwriter, YouTube Vlogger, make-up artist, and gospel recording artist. With creativity at the core of my endeavors, I've contributed to renowned magazines like Mogul Leaders Magazine, N.B.Q Magazine, and K.I.S.H. Magazine. As the visionary behind B.A.B.Y. Ministry, I aspire to save souls, heal marriages, and break chains. My coaching approach centers on clarity, goal setting, and actionable plans for success.

Dr. Lashawnda Love

📞 334-232-9281

✉️ lashawndashiree@gmail.com

🌐 www.lashawndashiree.info

Packages start at

$499

I repair credit
ASK ME HOW?

WE HELP REMOVE

- ✓ REPOSSESSIONS
- ✓ STUDENT LOANS
- ✓ LATE PAYMENTS
- ✓ COLLECTIONS
- ✓ CHARGE-OFFS
- ✓ CHILD SUPPORT
- ✓ EVICTIONS

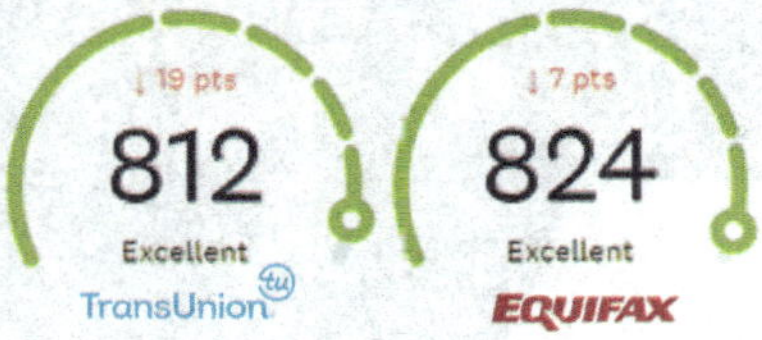

- ✓ FORECLOSURES
- ✓ JUDGEMENTS
- ✓ TAX LIENS
- ✓ SHORT SALES
- ✓ MEDICAL BILLS
- ✓ PUBLIC RECORDS
- ✓ AND MANY MORE

↓ 19 pts — 812 Excellent TransUnion
↓ 7 pts — 824 Excellent EQUIFAX

TEXT CREDIT CONSULT FOR FURTHER DETAILS AT (470)-453-1092.

NEED A 501C3?

Do It Yourself

WHAT'S INSIDE:
- **STEP-BY-STEP** INSTRUCTIONS FOR COMPLETING AND SUBMITTING FORM 1023-EZ.
- **PRE-FILLED EXAMPLE** FORMS FOR CLARITY AND ACCURACY.
- LINKS TO ESSENTIAL IRS RESOURCES.
- TIPS FOR MAINTAINING **TAX-EXEMPT STATUS.**
- BONUS CONTENT TO SUPPORT YOUR NONPROFIT'S SUCCESS.

EMAIL INTELLECTUALDESIGNS20@GMAIL.COM

Larry & Felisha Draggs
Strong Love, Simple Moments

"Strong Love, Simple Moments: The Real Journey of Larry & Felisha Draggs"

Some love stories begin with a whisper, others with a double take—and for Felisha Draggs, it was definitely the latter. "I was riding by the Village Pantry Store with a friend," she recalls. "And I saw this tall, dark man in a white tank, grey joggers, and white sneakers... OH MY GOD. I had to spin the block and get his number!" she laughs. That moment? Pure destiny.

Now, 21 years together and 15 years married, Larry and Felisha Draggs have built a marriage rooted in real love, deep laughter, and unshakable strength. Their connection didn't just grow over time—it was nurtured with intention, honesty, and a whole lot of rides around town listening to old school classics.

What made Felisha fall in love? "His smile, his honesty, and the way he loved my children," she says without hesitation. For them, love wasn't just about sparks—it was about safety, support, and showing up.

> "It's the small things—laughing, riding, talking—that keep us happy and going." – Felisha Draggs

If they had to describe their marriage in one word, it would be STRONG. Not just because of the years they've shared, but because of what they've overcome. One of their biggest challenges was learning to heal individually while still growing together as one. It wasn't easy—but they chose communication over silence. "We created a safe space to talk things out," Felisha shares. "That made all the difference."

Dragg's

Their favorite thing to do together? Riding around town with oldie goldie music playing, windows down, joy riding like teenagers in love. "It's the small things," Felisha says, "the laughing, the talking, those are the moments that keep us going."

To keep the love alive, they still date each other. "Even after all these years, we make time for each other. You have to," she says. "That's how you keep it fresh."

And if they could tell newlyweds one thing? It would be this: "Keep others out of your marriage." Protect what's sacred. Nurture what's real. And keep your home covered in prayer.

Speaking of prayer, their daily petition is simple but powerful: to love, communicate, and grow stronger together. That prayer has carried them through the storms and into seasons of joy they never thought possible.

When it comes to favorite memories, it's not about big vacations or flashy gifts. "It's the everyday moments—riding around laughing and talking," Felisha says. "Those are the memories that mean the most."

Larry and Felisha Draggs are living proof that strong love isn't about perfection—it's about presence. It's about showing up, holding on, and making even the ordinary feel unforgettable.

LARRY & FELISHA *Draggs*

"We created a safe space to talk things out—and that made all the difference."

– FELISHA DRAGGS

DRAGGS REAL QUICK

Met: Village Pantry Store
Together: 21 years
Married: 15 years
Nicknames: Lee Lee and Bootie
Favorite Memory: Riding around town, laughing and talking
Marriage Word: STRONG
Daily Prayer: To love, communicate, and keep our marriage stronger

VIOLA MARIE FLANDERS

Viola Marie Flanders is a beloved figure in Bainbridge, Georgia, known for her infectious laughter, nurturing spirit, and unwavering dedication to her family and community. Born to the late Virginia Fudge and Willie B. Jackson, Viola has embraced her roles as wife, mother, grandmother, and community leader with grace and joy.

Married to Ervin Flanders for 51 years, Viola has been a steadfast partner, embodying the role of a devoted wife, which she dreamed of since childhood. Together, they have raised five children: Stanley Flanders (Lashaun), Tiffany Jones (Willie), Lashawnda Love (David), Sharika Ausgood (Victor), and the late Ervin Flanders Jr. Her legacy extends through her 17 grandchildren, who adore her as "Big Vi" and cherish the warmth and laughter she brings into their lives.

Viola is renowned for her comedic talent, always able to bring joy and laughter to those around her. Her sense of humor is a hallmark of her personality, making her a cherished friend and confidante to many. She is also a talented decorator and fashion enthusiast, known for her stylish makeup, hair, and lashes.

"She has mastered the role of a devoted wife, which she dreamed of since childhood."

A LIFE OF LAUGHTER, LOVE, AND SERVICE

"Her ministry has touched countless lives, providing spiritual guidance and support to many in her community."

Beyond her family, Viola has dedicated 18 years to her faith journey, co-pastoring at God's Temple with her husband, Pastor Ervin Flanders. She founded the Wailing Women ministry, which has been instrumental in nurturing many prophets, prophetesses, evangelists, preachers, and teachers over its 21 years. Her ministry has touched countless lives, providing spiritual guidance and support to many in her community.

Viola's talents extend to her hands-on skills as a master seamstress, altering clothing for many in Bainbridge. Her nurturing nature is evident not only in her care for people but also in her love for animals, often tending to sick pets and stray animals, nursing them back to health.

Known for her culinary skills, Viola's cooking is celebrated by all who have had the pleasure of tasting her dishes. Her ability to create delicious meals adds another layer to her already multifaceted persona.

Viola Marie Flanders is a woman of many names—Big Vi, Nana, Mama, Vi-lonely-Gal—but no matter what she is called, her presence is a blessing to all who know her. She is an aunt, sister, amazing friend, and dedicated prayer partner, whose laughter, love, and service continue to light up every room she enters.

"UNVEILING DESTINY:
The Faith-Fueled Journey of Stacie Rogers"

Stacie

My name is Stacie Rogers, and I am filled with joy as I share my journey with you. I wear many hats in life, for I am not only a paralegal and a certified early childhood teacher, but also an Evangelist of the gospel. My heart's desire is to spread the love of God to all who will listen.

In addition to my professional roles, I am the proud CEO of Juliette catering service, where I strive to serve others with excellence. However, my true passion lies in serving the Lord and being a vessel of His grace. With God's guidance, I have been able to accomplish extraordinary things.

As a mother of four children and grandmother to seven precious grandchildren, my heart overflows with gratitude for the blessings bestowed upon me. Through all the ups and downs, I have learned to lean on the promises of God and find strength in His Word.

I am a devoted member of God's Temple of Holy Praise 2, where I find solace and encouragement among fellow believers. One scripture that I hold dear to my heart is Philippians 4:13, which says, "I can do all things through Christ who strengthens me." This verse reminds me that no matter the challenge, I can overcome it with God's help.

My faith is not dependent on what I see with my physical eyes, but on the unwavering trust I have in the Lord. As 2 Corinthians 5:7 tells us, "For we walk by faith, not by sight." This verse has become my guiding light, leading me through every step of my journey.

Prayer is the foundation of my life. I find great joy in interceding for others, knowing that God hears and answers our prayers. I believe in treating others with kindness and love, just as I would want to be treated. The golden rule of loving my neighbor as myself resonates deeply within me.

While I am single at the moment, I eagerly await the unfolding of my destiny in the King. As I continue to trust in God's perfect timing, I am reminded of Jeremiah 29:11, which assures me, "For I know the plans I have for you, plans to prosper you and not to harm you, plans to give you hope and a future."

In conclusion, I am Stacie Rogers, a woman who loves God and seeks to serve Him faithfully. Through the power of scripture and the grace of God, I live a life filled with purpose and excitement. I am confident that with Christ by my side, I can conquer any obstacle that comes my way.

Meet Delesa Patterson

A POWERFUL FORCE OF FAITH AND EMPOWERMENT

ABOUT HER

DR. DELESA PATTERSON

Delesa Patterson is a woman whose life is deeply rooted in faith, and her passion for empowering others shines through everything she does. From her humble beginnings in Tallulah, Louisiana, to her current role as a leader and teacher of faith, Delesa's journey is nothing short of extraordinary.

Growing up in Tallulah, Delesa attended Tallulah High School, where her natural drive and commitment helped her excel. She went on to pursue higher education at Restoration Theological Seminary in Jonesboro, Georgia, where she earned her Master's in Theology and a Doctorate in Religious Philosophy. With these accomplishments under her belt, Delesa founded Kingdom Leaders Seminary, a fully accredited institution that continues to shape the next generation of leaders in faith.

DELESA'S PERSONALITY IS A PERFECT MIX OF JOY AND PURPOSE.

Though she's outgoing and social, she also has a more introverted, thoughtful side. With a Sanguine and Phlegmatic temperament, she brings a balance of warmth and wisdom to every interaction. Whether she's enjoying a game of pool, spades, or dominoes, or laughing along to her favorite comedy, Delesa's zest for life is contagious.

But it's her deep commitment to her Kingdom Assignment that truly defines Delesa. As a Christian Counselor and Family Therapist, she founded The Home of The Good Shepherd Ministries in Atlanta back in 2001, where she served as a pastor for 21 years. Her love for people and desire to help them overcome challenges has been a guiding force throughout her life. In 2015, she expanded her mission with Matters of the Heart Christian Counseling and Family Therapy, offering holistic support to families in need.

In 2016, Delesa took on another major role by leading Kingdom Ambassadors Ministries in Thomasville, Georgia. Her influence stretches back to 1985 when she became a licensed missionary at Peter Rock Baptist Church in Ft. Hood, Texas, inspired by her mentors, Reverend Willie Hardy Jr. and Mother Evangelist Gloria Hardy Fountain.

Beyond her work in ministry and counseling, Delesa is a devoted mother of three sons and a proud grandmother of six. She enjoys reading, listening to a variety of music genres like gospel, jazz, classical, and R&B, and living life with a sense of adventure. Her love for speed and thrill-seeking adds an exciting dimension to her already inspiring story.

Delesa's life is a testament to what it means to live fully in faith and purpose. Whether she's teaching, counseling, or simply spreading joy, she is a beacon of empowerment for all those around her. Her goal is clear: to "plunder Hell and populate Heaven," a mission she approaches with unwavering commitment. Get ready to be inspired by this dynamic leader whose journey continues to impact countless lives.

LET ME PROMOTE YOUR *Book*

More exposure!! More sells!!

THE LOVE LAB
DESIGN & PUBLISHING CO.

BUILT WITH PASSION.
BRANDED BY PURPOSE.

HARMONY HYMNS

LADYFREEJEWELS
Freontae MAYNOR

My Start (The Journey Continues)

Freontae Patrice Maynor a.k.a. better known as "Free" is the daughter of Fred Maynor and Elder Patricia A. Maynor. Freontae started singing at a very young age in the St. John P.B. Church youth choir under the direction of Pastor Gwen Lockwood and her mother. Only a few years later her passion for the piano developed and she started playing for her very first church at the age of seven. Over the years Freontae fell in love with praise & worship. Freontae recognized that she have been chosen to lead the people of God into the very presence of the almighty. She's had many opportunities and privileges of traveling the world as a backup singing for such artists as Fantasia, Dave Hollister, Donnie McClurkin, Vashawn Mitchell and many more. "Free" is more than a worship leader. She has been chosen as well to preach the gospel of Jesus Christ. Freontae motto is to "make God Famous only" and that He may be glorified anytime and anywhere. Freontae released her first single, "Walk By Faith" (available on all digital outlets) in Sept 2019 and currently working on new music. She is the proud CEO of online jewelry boutique, Lady Free Jewels. Freontae is currently works for Harborview Medical Center in Seattle, Washington as an Sterile Processing Technician II. Freontae is currently a proud member of The Rhema Church of Atlanta where Dr. Gabriel Allen Powell is the pastor.
www.ladyfreejewels.com

K. FREE & FREE FLOW

A New Wave of Worship

K. Free & Free Flow is an amazing group of singers hailing from different southern counties in Georgia. Back in 2018, their founder had a powerful vision. She wanted to create a group that could connect with the younger generation and those who often feel left out or rejected by both society and the church.

Gathering a group of passionate young adults, she launched the Free Flow Prophetic Worship Conference at Redeeming Life Fellowship Church in Cairo, GA. That's where it all began! The founder soon realized that this wasn't just a one-time event; there was a bigger mission ahead. They envisioned traveling and creating a unique sound that could reach and inspire all souls.

The group features a talented lineup of vocalists, including sopranos and altos, as well as a tenor. They're currently working hard on their very first EP album, and the excitement is building! Mark your calendars for January 18, 2025, when they will host their live recording. Plus, they have some special guest artists lined up to join them, making it an event you won't want to miss!

So, keep an eye on K. Free & Free Flow as they make big moves in the music world. Their mission is all about uplifting spirits and spreading love through their music!

Lashawnda SHIREE
I AM ME

Download Now

DEEZER amazon

Spotify TIDAL

NEW BOOK

FRUIT OF THE SPIRIT

AUTHOR
Dr. Lashawnda Love

AVAILABLE ON AMAZON → **GET YOUR COPY TODAY!**

DR. LASHAWNDA LOVE

I'M AVAILABLE

CONTACT ME TODAY

334-232-9281

- RECORDING ARTIST
- CONFERENCE HOST
- PRAISE AND WORSHIP
- MOTIVATIONAL SPEAKER
- PREACHER
- TEACHER

CONTACT ME TODAY

- www.lashawndashiree.com
- www.payhip.com/lashawndashiree
- intellectualdesigns20@gmail.com
- storkpublishingllc@gmail.com

Rising Stars

DARE TO BE DIFFERENT:
THE CREATIVE BRILLIANCE OF 11-YEAR-OLD
Germani Bromfield

At just 11 years old, Germani Bromfield is making waves in the fashion world straight out of Dallas, Georgia. As the creative force and CEO behind EarDropsByGermani, this young entrepreneur is already mastering her craft and building a brand on bold originality. What started with yarn and denim tassel earrings has blossomed into a full line of handcrafted denim neckties, purses, belts, and socks—all designed with a personal touch that sets her apart.

What started as a playful experiment with yarn and denim tassel earrings has blossomed into a thriving business rooted in creativity, style, and bold expression. "I had the vision, but I just couldn't get it quite right at first," Germani shares. "But now I do—thank God." With prayer, persistence, and a whole lot of passion, Germani has taken her ideas from sketches to statements.

Her signature denim neckties—each one uniquely adorned with rhinestones, pearls, and personality—are more than fashion pieces. They are wearable declarations of individuality. "My designs are original," Germani proudly explains. "No one will have the exact same tie as you. My mom always says, 'Dare to be different.' So that's what I do."

But Germani's talent doesn't stop there. She also designs denim purses, belts, and socks—each one handmade with love and flair. From her humble beginnings to the polished pieces she now creates, Germani's journey is a testimony of growth. "This was when I first started doing the denim necktie—I've really made progress," she says with joy.

Her website, www.eardropsbygermani.com, showcases her full line and reflects the fearless creativity behind her brand. Keep your eyes on this young mogul—she's not only crafting fashion, she's building a future!

Purpose Lovel Lamb

Meet Purpose Lovel Lamb, a bright, talented, and purpose-driven young star from Bainbridge, Georgia. Her name says it all—Purpose—a divine assignment straight from God. Her parents were led by the Holy Spirit to give her that name, and she continues to live up to it every single day.

This young trailblazer has already made waves online, becoming a viral TikTok sensation after her dance video in the famous silver pants racked up over 1.1 million views and counting. On Facebook, she and her favorite cousin form a dynamic duo, entertaining and inspiring with fun, family-friendly dance videos that have reached over 1.9 million views.

Beyond social media, Purpose shines in every area she touches. She's a cheerleader, basketball player, and member of the Stomp Team at Bainbridge Middle School, where she was recently nominated for 6th Grade Homecoming Court—a proud moment made even more special as she was escorted by her father, Willie Lamb Jr.

Purpose's creativity doesn't stop there. She's an author and young entrepreneur, inspiring her generation through faith-filled books that celebrate confidence, joy, and identity. Her titles include:

- Hey, My Name Is Purpose Lamb and I Love My Hair! (Activity Book)
- Girl's Purpose on Purpose Affirmation Journal
- He Woke You Up On Purpose Journal
- Get Ready With Me: A Birthday Coloring Book — her newest release, celebrating the fun and faith of growing up with purpose and positivity.

In addition to her athletic and academic pursuits, Purpose also trains at Future Stars Training Center, where she hones her skills in gymnastics and lyrical dancing—a reflection of her grace, discipline, and dedication to excellence.
Though she's accomplished so much at such a young age, this is only the beginning. The journey of Purpose Lovel Lamb is one of faith, family, creativity, and confidence. Her light continues to shine bright, inspiring other young girls to love themselves, chase their dreams, and live every day on purpose.

Stay tuned, because the best is yet to come.

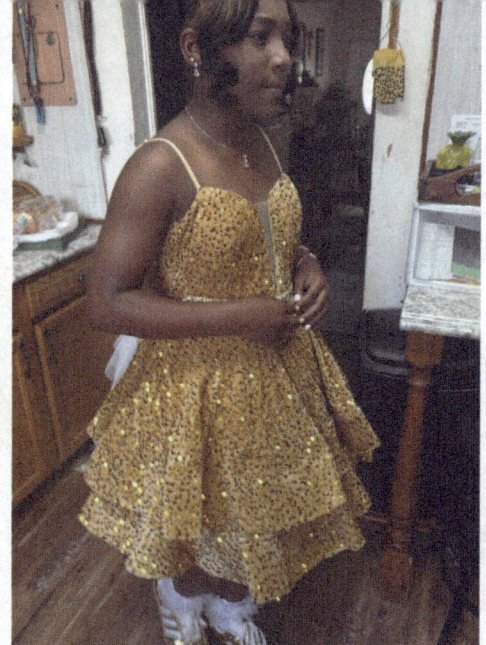

NEW BOOK

GET READY WITH ME
"A BIRTHDAY COLORING BOOK"

AUTHOR
Purpose Lovel Lamb

AVAILABLE ON AMAZON — GET YOUR COPY TODAY!

BOOK RELEASE

Hey, My Name is Purpose Lamb, and I LOVE MY HAIR!
PURPOSE LOVEL LAMB

Hey, My Name is Purpose Lamb and I Love My Hair
Activity Book and Journal

AUTHOR
Purpose Lamb

NEW RELEASE
BOOK BY
Malaysia Thomas

Who Can I Tell?
by Malaysia Thomas

AVAILABLE FOR PURCHASE AT
amazon — https://payhip.com/MalaysiaBabes

OUT OF THE MOUTH OF BABES

Malaysia Thomas is God's chosen servant and the epitome of Jeremiah 1:5: "Before I formed you in the womb I knew you; Before you were born I sanctified you; I ordained you a prophet to the nations." Malaysia is six years old and has been used by God in more ways than most adults. She is the Lord's Mouthpiece, Prophet, Intercessor, Worshipper, Watchman, Author, CEO, and Entrepreneur. From infancy and continuously, Malaysia has been in training in accordance with Proverbs 22:6: "Train up a child in the way he should go, and when he is old, he will not depart from it." It is so important to have a solid foundation built on the word and principles of God. Malaysia has been a part of Out of the Mouth of Babes outreach ministries from infancy and is also being trained as a leader. She has been out with the ministry and in the communities as a baby, and her presence and the fragrance she carries of the Father have touched souls. Malaysia serves the ministry in many ways and has made an impact with God's people.

Here are a few examples:

Community Outreach: Malaysia helps impact the community by assisting the ministry with passing out food and water to families and the homeless. She helps distribute toiletries, personal and household items, and whatever the ministry can obtain for the people. She also prays with and for the people.

Back to School Bash: Malaysia assists the ministry at the back-to-school bash with passing out backpacks, school supplies, shoes, and whatever the ministry acquires for the children. This is especially beneficial for parents who are less fortunate or are experiencing financial difficulties.

Nursing Home Outreach: Malaysia assists with the nursing home outreach by handing out gifts of blankets and socks to the elderly during the Christmas holidays. The love of Christ inside Malaysia brings joy and smiles to His people.

Christmas Toy Drive: Malaysia assists us every year with passing out toys to the children.

Malaysia has a phenomenal prayer life and is an intercessor. Her spirit is sharp, and the gift of discernment upon her life is powerful. She is in tune with the Holy Spirit, and God uses her to pray and cover her mother and brothers and release the word of the Lord. She makes up a hedge and stands in the gap for her family.

Malaysia is a CEO, entrepreneur, and author. She has released three books, has her own lip gloss brands, and Cutie Patootie Hair Bonnets.

First Book: Malaysia's Journal and Activity Book.

Second Book: Who Can I Tell?

Third Book: Malaysia's Week of Hallelujah Anyhow.

Malaysia currently has four lip gloss products. Babes Psalm 8:2 Lip Gloss includes the following brands: Crush Lip Gloss, Diamonds & Pearls Lip Gloss, Sock It to Me Pink Lip Gloss, and Yummy Lip Gloss. And let us not forget Malaysia's Cutie Patootie Hair Bonnets in beautiful pink colors.

Malaysia's products can be found on the following websites:

Amazon https://amzn.to/4afllxS or Search Malaysia Thomas Books.
PayHip: https://payhip.com/b/hL4NG (Book, Lip-glosses & Hair Bonnets)

This is just the beginning for this young and gifted servant of God, CEO, entrepreneur, and author. Her potential is limitless, for the God she serves is without limits. There is much more to come forth from Malaysia Thomas, and as we can see, age will not be a factor for God's anointed one. She is most definitely needed for such a time as this.hiping God.

Malaysia Thomas

Journal/Activity Book

Lip Gloss Line

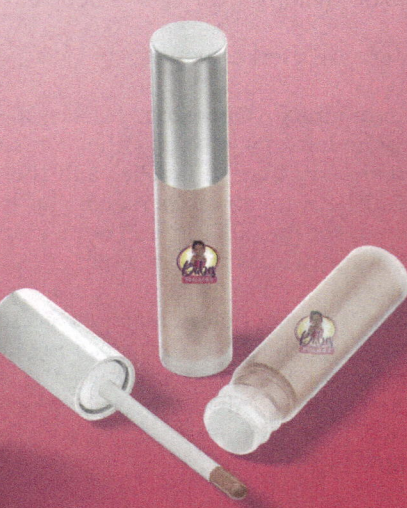

AVAILABLE FOR PURCHASE AT
amazon https://payhip.com/MalaysiaBabes

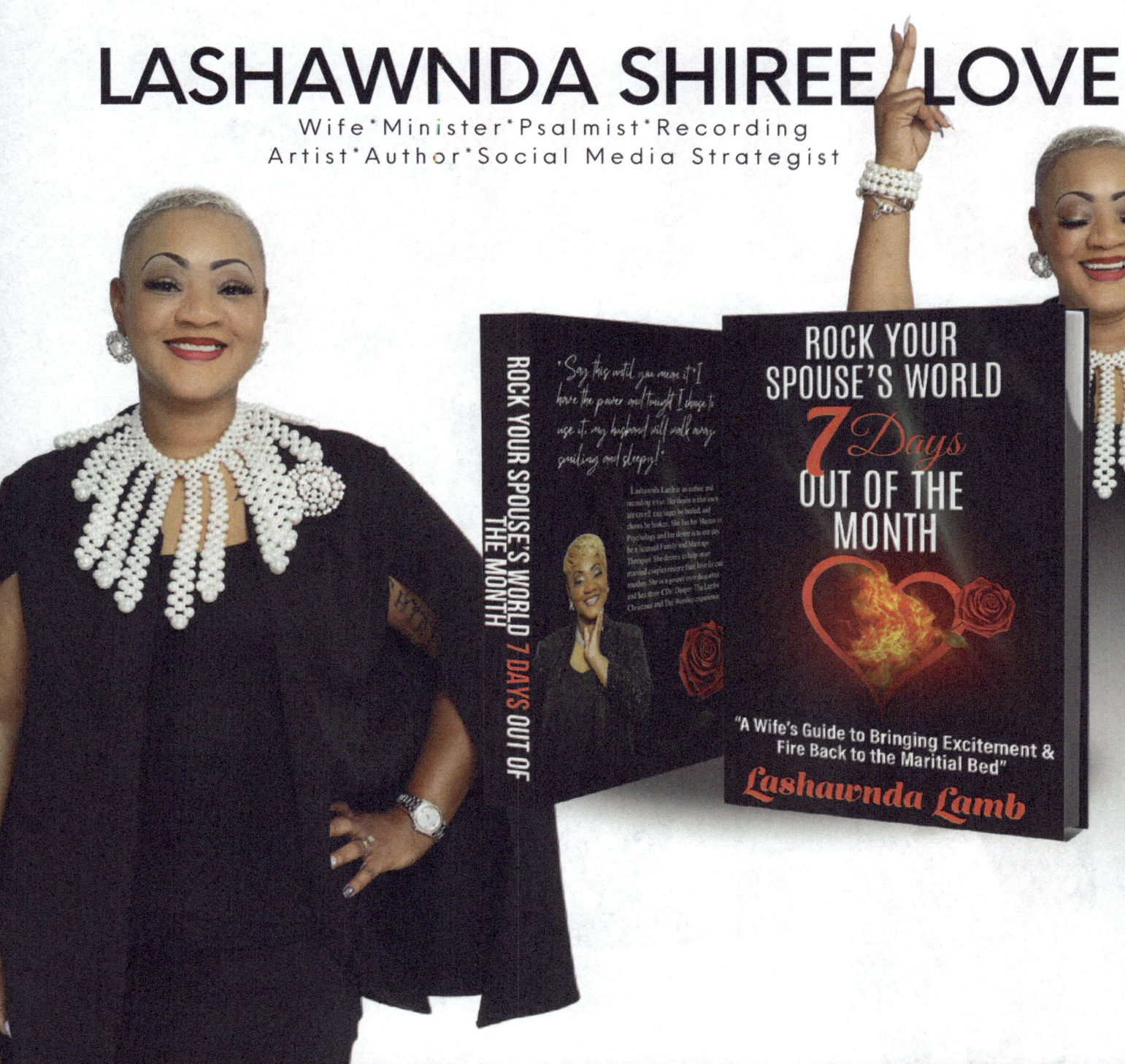

MORE BOOKS & RESOURCES BY DR. LASHAWNDA SHIREE LOVE

Explore more faith-based tools, journals, devotionals, and empowerment books written by Dr. Lashawnda Shiree Love—each one designed to equip, encourage, and help you grow in purpose, healing, and identity.

Order now on Amazon

Order now on Amazon

Order now on Amazon

Order now on Amazon

Order now on Amazon

Order now on Amazon

Order now on Amazon

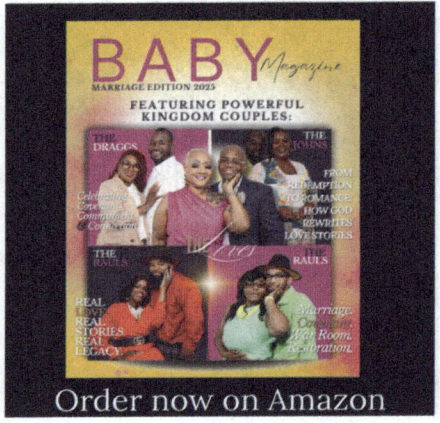
Order now on Amazon

Order now on Amazon

Order now on Amazon

Order now on Amazon

Order now on Amazon

Order now on Amazon

Order now on Amazon

Order now on Amazon

Order now on Amazon

Order now on Amazon

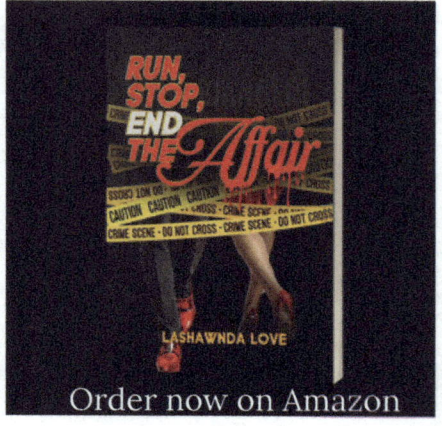
Order now on Amazon

Order now on Amazon

Order now on Amazon

Download for free

NEW BOOK

RUN, STOP END THE AFFAIR

AUTHOR
Dr. Lashawnda Love

AVAILABLE ON AMAZON
GET YOUR COPY TODAY!

Made in the USA
Coppell, TX
07 January 2026